# ROLLER DERBY RIVALS

by **Sue Macy**

*illustrated by* **Matt Collins**

Holiday House / New York

# ROLLER DERBY RULES, 1948

Each team consists of five men and five women.

Men skate against men.

Women skate against women.

Games are divided into eight 15-minute periods, alternating between men and women.

Both teams skate around the track.

To score, a skater breaks away from the pack, circles the track, and then passes members of the other team. Her team gets one point for every opponent she passes.

A scoring play is called a jam.

The scorer is a jammer.

Referees can send skaters to the penalty box for tripping, holding, fighting, and unnecessary roughness.

*Crash!*

Midge "Toughie" Brasuhn teeters off-balance
as Gerry Murray smashes into her.
Gerry's fans roar their approval
of the graceful Roller Derby queen,
while the short, scrappy Toughie fumes.
Arms flailing, feet skidding in her wobbly skates,
Toughie finally flops down hard on the wooden track.
It's a toss-up what hurts more, her pride or her behind.

Today is December 5, 1948, and
close to five thousand people
are packed into New York's 69th Regiment Armory
for Roller Derby, the newest game in town.

Each night, male and female skaters try to score points
by breaking away from the pack, circling the track,
and passing their opponents.
While everyone skates with guts and determination,
it's the women who drive the crowds wild.

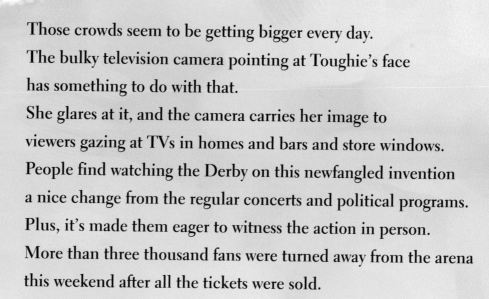

Those crowds seem to be getting bigger every day.
The bulky television camera pointing at Toughie's face
has something to do with that.
She glares at it, and the camera carries her image to
viewers gazing at TVs in homes and bars and store windows.
People find watching the Derby on this newfangled invention
a nice change from the regular concerts and political programs.
Plus, it's made them eager to witness the action in person.
More than three thousand fans were turned away from the arena
this weekend after all the tickets were sold.

Now everyone in the stands is yelling
for Toughie to get back in the game.
She struggles to her feet and joins her team,
picking up speed as she skates down the banked track.
Toughie sees Gerry circling the oval, trying to score.
She falls back, waits for Gerry, and
crashes into her side with a perfectly timed slam.

"Foul!" shouts a woman in the stands.
"You're a bum, Toughie Brasuhn!"
Toughie didn't sign on to be the Derby's villain,
but that appears to be her fate.
Her rough, street-fighter looks make her
the perfect foil for a glamour girl like Gerry.
No matter that her redheaded rival
has just as many dirty tricks up her sleeve as Toughie.
It seems that all Gerry has to do is flash her pearly whites
and the referees go blind to her transgressions.

That's not the only reason Gerry has an advantage.
This Roller Derby troupe is divided into two teams
that travel around the county playing each other.
Gerry always skates for the Home team
and Toughie for the Visitors.
During this seventeen-day run in Manhattan,
the arena belongs to Gerry's New York squad.
Toughie and her Brooklyn team are the enemies.
But that just makes Toughie fight harder.
The more people root against her,
the more fired up she gets.

Tonight, Toughie is plenty fired up.
She rolls right through the pack of New York skaters,
pushing aside anyone who's in her path.
The jam is on.
Toughie speeds all the way around the track,
bracing for the moment she will catch up
to her New York rivals and try to pass them.
Up ahead, she sees her Brooklyn teammates
jostling the New Yorkers to make room for her.
She passes an opponent to score one point for Brooklyn
and then . . .

*Smash!*

Gerry rams Toughie hard toward the padded railing
at the top of the banked track.
Toughie catches the railing, but she's going too fast.
She flips right over it and lands
in the aisle next to the front row of seats.

"Way to go, Gerry!" cries a man somewhere behind her.
His taunt brings on a chorus of cheers
and a stream of balled-up paper thrown at Toughie.
She climbs back on the track quickly,
before anyone can douse her with a cup of soda.

Toughie can thank Leo Seltzer
for the extreme reactions she gets from fans.
Leo runs the Derby. He founded it back in the 1930s.
And he set up Toughie as the skater fans love to hate.
Before the Derby got to New York last week,
Leo plastered the city with billboards and posters
asking the question, "Who Is Toughie?"
The answer was a photograph of her at her meanest,
with a dirty face and tousled hair,
wearing a Roller Derby jersey.

Everyone in the arena is about to see exactly who Toughie is.
She grits her teeth as she rejoins her teammates
and breaks from the pack for another jam.
This time Gerry breaks with her.
They race around the track, egging on the crowd and
bumping each other when they skate past the TV cameras.
Whenever Gerry tries to get ahead, Toughie also speeds up.
Finally, Toughie lowers her shoulder and rams her rival,
sending her flying toward the Home team's bench.
The male skaters on the bench scatter like bowling pins.

Gerry dusts herself off and catches up with Toughie.

For the briefest moment both skaters grin.

Fans would be shocked to learn that the two women,

sworn enemies on the track,

actually get along just fine.

After all, they need each other.

Every hero needs a villain.

And every villain needs a worthy opponent.

Gerry hammers that point home when she jabs an elbow

into Toughie's ribs and knocks her off her feet.

## Author's Note

In 1949, several Roller Derby audiences in New York City answered a questionnaire that asked how they had first heard about the Derby. A whopping 79 percent said they first saw it on TV. That statistic was reported in a June 4, 1949, article in *Business Week* that was appropriately titled "Roller Derby—an Industry Made by Television." The next day, *New York Times* TV critic Jack Gould wrote that "the derby was a flop until television made it an accepted way of life in pub and parlor."

While television coverage increased the popularity of Roller Derby, the Derby also helped establish television's appeal as an entertainment medium. In fact, according to Harry Coyle, a longtime director at NBC, "Television got off the ground because of sports." In 1948, the nascent TV industry needed programming, and sports provided a few solid hours of unpredictable, engaging spectacle. Boxing, wrestling, and Roller Derby were especially appealing because they took place indoors and in a confined area, so camera operators could control the lighting and focus on the faces of the participants as well as the action. That was not the case with baseball, football, and other sports played in outdoor stadiums.

Jack Gould sarcastically wrote that Roller Derby was evidence that "the hours of toil which the scientists spent in developing television were not wasted." If critics such as Gould were on the fence about the inherent value of the Derby, no one questioned the athletic ability of its female stars. In 1950, US sportswriters voted Toughie Brasuhn one of the ten outstanding women in sports. A 1958 *New York Times* profile of Gerry Murray described her as "a female terror, swishing around the track at thirty-five miles an hour, hipping her opponents and zigzagging recklessly, her red hair, tied in a ribbon, winging along behind her." The appreciation of female Roller Derby stars by male sportswriters was all the more noteworthy because the public image of American women had taken a decidedly domestic turn after World War II.

Instead of ferrying airplanes and building ships, many middle-class women were now raising families in new suburban homes. The bruising, brawling women of Roller Derby were a throwback to the raucous war years, when women's achievements knew no bounds.

Perhaps inevitably, the Roller Derby life took a toll on some skaters. Toughie Brasuhn suffered two broken collarbones and eight broken noses during her stint in the Derby. She died of unrelated causes in 1971, at age forty-eight. But as of this writing, her worthiest opponent, Gerry Murray, was ninety-three years old and living in Iowa. Gerry's son, Mike Gammon, was a Roller Derby star in his own right from the 1950s to the 1980s.

### An Important Notice from the Author and Illustrator

Thanks to press coverage and interviews given by various Roller Derby stars, we know quite a bit about the Roller Derby's seventeen-day run in New York City late in 1948. But since no TV footage or play-by-play narrative of the December 5 match portrayed in this book survives, we have done our best to re-create it as realistically as possible. All dialogue and skating action are dramatizations based on our research.

# Roller Derby Time Line

**1935** Leo Seltzer creates the Transcontinental Roller Derby, a marathon race in which teams of one man and one woman skate around a banked track for days on end.

**1937** Seltzer's organization is almost destroyed when twenty-one Roller Derby skaters and officials perish in a bus crash.

**1938** Sportswriter Damon Runyon watches Roller Derby and suggests that the game needs a scoring system and more contact between skaters. Seltzer reimagines it as a competition between two teams of five men and five women.

**1946** Roller Derby is televised locally in New York City, but only about 8,000 households in the area have TVs.

**1948** Roller Derby holds a seventeen-day run in New York City that is televised locally. By now at least 172,000 US households have TVs, most of them in the New York area.

**1949** Seltzer forms the National Roller Derby League (NRDL) with six teams. The league's World Series is held at Madison Square Garden in New York.

**1950** Mickey Rooney stars in *The Fireball*, a feature film about an orphan who makes it big in Roller Derby before being stricken with polio. Marilyn Monroe has a bit part.

**1952** The Roller Derby Hall of Fame is established.

**1958** Leo Seltzer's son Jerry takes over day-to-day operation of the Roller Derby.

**1960s** After the Roller Derby starts showing its videotaped matches on national TV, Derby road tours sell out at arenas across the country.

**1961** The National Skating Derby is formed as a rival to the NRDL. Its matches are called Roller Games.

**1971** *Derby*, a documentary film, looks at one man's attempt to break into the sport.

**1972** Raquel Welch stars in *Kansas City Bomber*, a feature film about the romantic and professional life of a Roller Derby star.

**1973** Jim Croce releases his album *Life and Times*, featuring the song "Roller Derby Queen." Also, Jerry Seltzer sells the original Roller Derby to the National Skating Derby.

**1989** The syndicated TV series *Roller Games* airs for one season.

**1999** *Roller Jam*, a TV series about a fictional Roller Derby league, premiers on The Nashville Network (TNN). It runs for two years.

**Early 2000s** Roller Derby enjoys a revival as women's amateur and semipro leagues crop up all over the United States.

**2006** From January through March, the A&E TV network broadcasts *Rollergirls*, a reality series focusing on the Austin, Texas, Lonestar Rollergirls Roller Derby league. By August there are more than 135 women's Derby leagues in the United States.

**2009** Drew Barrymore directs and stars in the feature film *Whip It*, about a present-day Texas misfit who finds meaning in her life through Roller Derby.

**2011** Team USA survives a field of thirteen to win the first Roller Derby World Cup.

**2012** The International Olympic Committee announces that Roller Derby is one of eight new sports they are considering for the 2020 Summer Olympics.

## Sources and Resources

I started the research for this book by combing through spools of microfilm for New York City newspapers from mid-November through late December 1948 in search of every mention of Roller Derby I could find. This was an era when New York had close to a dozen daily newspapers, so there was a lot to look through. I was happy to learn that the *New York Times* reported the scores and attendance of the Roller Derby matches most days; and the *New York Journal-American* offered news articles, columns, photographs, and player profiles throughout the seventeen-day run. The *New York Sun* pitched in with a thoughtful article every few days, and the *Daily Mirror, Daily News,* and *World-Telegram* each offered a piece or two. Taken together, the reporting provided an excellent foundation for the other research I did on Roller Derby, the history of television, and New York City in the late 1940s. Citations for specific quotations and statistics can be found in the source notes on page 31.

Fortunately, there are a lot of Roller Derby resources that are easier to access than newspaper microfilm. Here are some of them.

### FILM CLIPS

YouTube has many examples of archival footage from 1940s and '50s Roller Derby matches. Among those worth watching are:

**"Presenting Roller Derby,"** focusing on one period of a 1950s Roller Derby match between the women of the Brooklyn Red Devils (Toughie's team) and the Chicago Westerners: www.youtube.com/watch?v=cMvwHg2ltbU.

**"Roller Derby,"** a 1950s clip featuring a five-lap "match race" during halftime of a Roller Derby game in which Gerry Murray and Loretta Behrens compete for $1,000: www.youtube.com/watch?v=XUzbTdZ2sP0.

**"Roller Derby Girl,"** a short 1949 film featuring Toughie Brasuhn and Jean Porter: www.youtube.com/watch?v=Nnf8wgmJFKI.

### WEB SITES

**Banked Track Memories**
www.bankedtrack.info
Perhaps the most valuable feature of this site is its collection of PDFs of programs and yearbooks from the Roller Derby and Roller Games, dating back to 1951. There are also many photographs of teams, games, and individual players, along with images of other artifacts from the sport's history.

**Roller Derby Hall of Fame**
www.rollerderbyhalloffame.com
This Web site is rich with photographs and information about the Roller Derby, from its beginnings in the 1930s to today. The site owner, Gary Powers, also has a memorabilia-packed hall of fame at his home in Brooklyn, New York. It's open to the public, by appointment only. For information, contact Gary at RollerDerbyHOF@aol.com.

### BOOKS

*Five Strides on the Banked Track: The Life and Times of the Roller Derby* by Frank Deford (Boston: Little, Brown and Company, 1971). The famed *Sports Illustrated* reporter presents the history of the sport, along with statistics and profiles of star skaters from the late 1960s. If you can find it, it's worth a look.

*Roller Derby to RollerJam: The Authorized Story of an Unauthorized Sport* by Keith Coppage (Santa Rosa, CA: Squarebooks, 1999). This beautiful volume, full of photographs and artifacts, is jam-packed with anecdotes about the Derby and its stars. The author, an admitted fan, worked for Derby guru Jerry Seltzer for a decade.

## SOURCE NOTES

Page

6   "close to five thousand people . . . the newest game in town": "New York Rollers Win, 13-11," *New York Times*, December 6, 1948.

9   "More than three thousand fans . . . were sold": "Skating," by Bill Love, *New York Journal-American*, December 7, 1948.

28  "79 percent . . . on TV": "Roller Derby—an Industry Made by Television," *Business Week*, June 4, 1949, pp. 22–24. The remaining audience members discovered Roller Derby through newspapers (9%), radio (8%), or discount tickets and passes (4%).

28  "the derby . . . and parlor": "The Roller Derby: Is It Television, Sport Or Narcotic?" by Jack Gould, *New York Times*, June 5, 1949.

28  "Television . . . because of sports": Quoted in "Sport in the Land of Television: The Use of Sport in Network Prime-Time Schedules, 1946–1950" by Jeff Neal-Lunsford, *Journal of Sport History*, Vol. 19, No. 1, Spring 1992: p. 59.

28  "the hours . . . not wasted": Gould, *ibid.*

28  "a female terror . . . behind her": "It's a Wonderful Whirl to Gerry," by Gay Talese, *New York Times*, October 10, 1958.

29  "Roller Derby . . . have TVs": Households with televisions, based on *Historical Statistics of the United States, Millennial Edition, Volume 4: Economic Sectors* (New York, Cambridge University Press, 2006): pp. 4–1027.

29  "By now . . . New York area": *ibid.*

## Acknowledgments

You couldn't grow up in the 1960s without watching Roller Derby on TV. And although the rivals of the day were Joanie Weston and Ann Calvello rather than earlier pioneers Toughie Brasuhn and Gerry Murray, I definitely got the message that women in the Roller Derby were just about the toughest athletes around. So thanks to those who skated back then for showing me that women can be strong and fearless. It's a lesson every girl should learn.

Thanks as well to all the people who offered support and advice as I worked on this book. That includes the folks at Holiday House, whose enthusiasm never wavered, especially Mary Cash, Sylvie Frank, Kelly Loughman, and Pam Glauber. It also includes my parents, brother, and friends, particularly Jackie Glasthal, to whom this book is dedicated. Her advice and encouragement always kept me on track. (Sorry about the pun.) Furthermore, I greatly appreciate the insights on Toughie and Gerry shared by Gary Powers of the National Roller Derby Hall of Fame. I was thrilled to attend the hall's 2012 induction ceremony and old-timers' game, where I sat in the front row and watched veteran stars hit the track and flip over the railing right before my very eyes. Apparently, age is not an impediment when the Derby is in your blood.

And finally, thanks to Matt Collins for capturing all the energy and personality of the early Roller Derby skaters in the wonderful illustrations that grace this book.          —S. M.

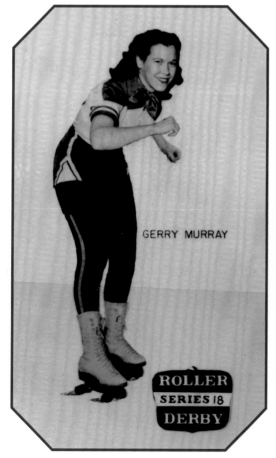

**Left: Gerry Murray, undated**

**Below: Toughie Brasuhn, 1948**

Both photos courtesy of the National Roller Derby Hall of Fame & Museum

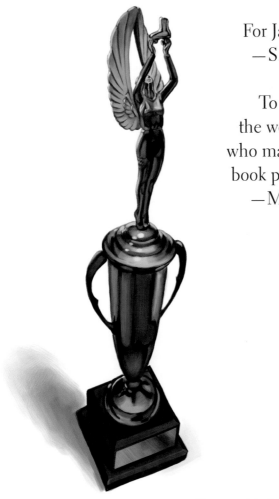

For Jackie
—S. M.

To all
the women
who made this
book possible
—M. C.

Text copyright © 2014 by Sue Macy
Illustrations copyright © 2014 by Matt Collins
All Rights Reserved
HOLIDAY HOUSE is registered in the U.S. Patent and Trademark Office.
Printed and Bound in April 2014
at Kwong Fat Offset Printing Co., Ltd., DongGuan City, China.
The artwork was created with Prismacolor pencils, Denril vellum,
Painter, and Adobe Photoshop.
www.holidayhouse.com
First Edition
1 3 5 7 9 10 8 6 4 2

Library of Congress Cataloging-in-Publication Data
Macy, Sue.
Roller derby rivals / by Sue Macy ; illustrated by Matt Collins. — First edition.
pages cm
ISBN 978-0-8234-2923-3 (hardcover)
1. Roller derbies—New York (State)—New York.
2. Roller derbies—United States. 3. Roller skaters—United States—Biography.
4. Women roller skaters—United States—Biography.
5. Brasuhn, Toughie, 1923-1971. 6. Murray, Gerry.
I. Collins, Matt, ill. II. Title.
GV859.6.M34 2014
796.2109747'1—dc23
2013001945